Tree Matters

Tree Matters

Copyright © 2014 Tara Books Private Limited
Illustrations by Gangu Bai
Text by Gita Wolf and V. Geetha from Gangu Bai's oral narrative

For this edition:
Tara Publishing Ltd., UK | www.tarabooks.com/uk
Tara Books Pvt. Ltd., India | www.tarabooks.com
Design: Jonathan Yamakami
Production: C. Arumugam
Printed in China by Leo Paper and Products.

ISBN 978-93-83145-23-2

Tree Matters

Illustrations by Gangu Bai

Text by Gita Wolf and V. Geetha from the oral narrative of Gangu Bai

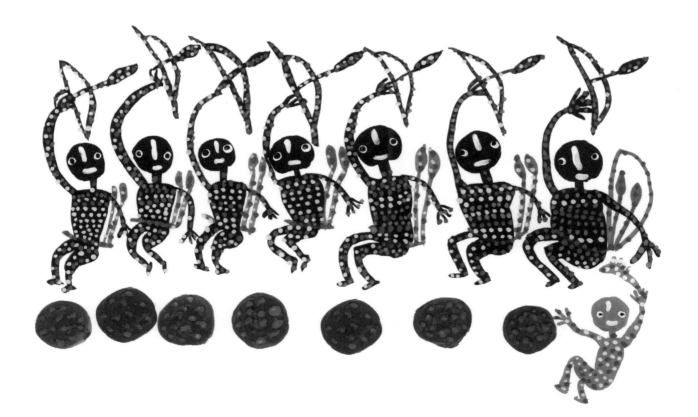

Between Field and Forest

The Bhils are one of the largest tribal communities in India. They live in villages between the field and the forest. They go into the jungle, but not as their ancestors did.

Earlier, the forest was a source of food — leaves, berries, fruits and seeds — a place to gather firewood, to rest or to play. Today, this is not easy, since there are rules about who may or may not go into a forest and what can be taken out of it.

But many Bhil people remember how it was.

Berries

Earlier, we grew some food for half a year. We didn't do anything the rest of the time.

You ate what you found, and drank water. You were lucky if you had one meal a day. Many people just survived eating berries from the forest. People didn't wear clothes like today, maybe just a piece of cloth tied around their waist.

Now things are a little different...

Now people farm for six months, and try to find work for the rest of the time. These days you need the money. But for the poor it is not easy. Poorer children from the village still eat berries for a meal. Many people still don't wear slippers or shoes, even in the forest.

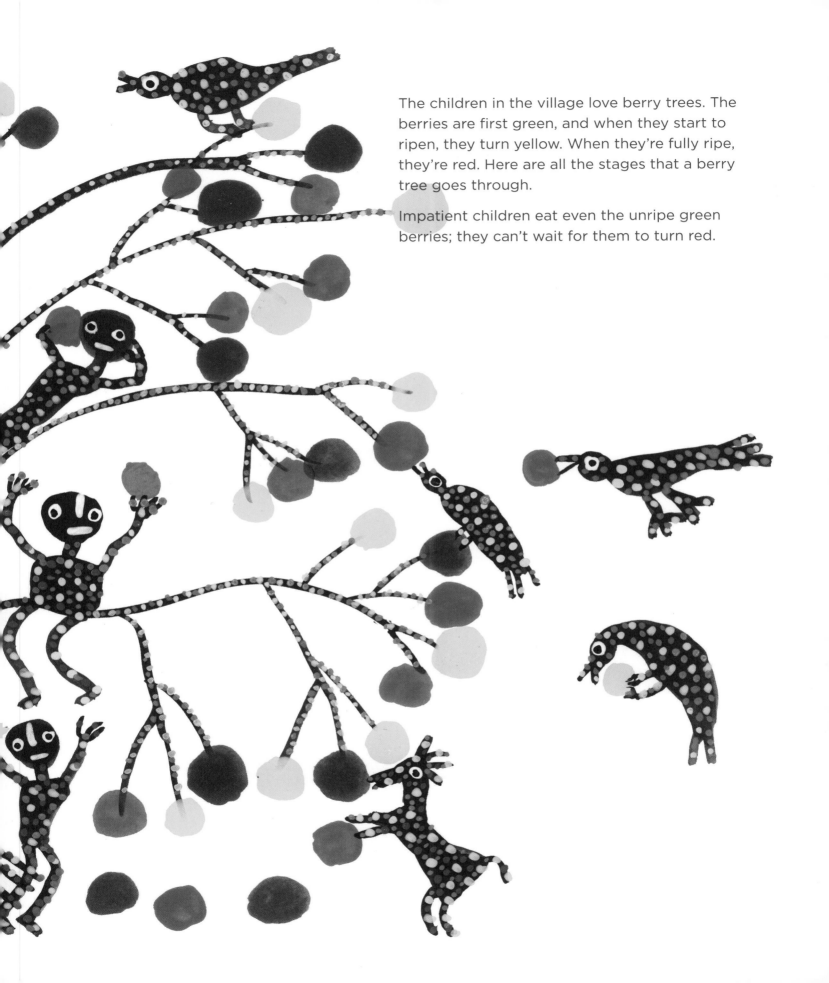

The children in the village love berry trees. The berries are first green, and when they start to ripen, they turn yellow. When they're fully ripe, they're red. Here are all the stages that a berry tree goes through.

Impatient children eat even the unripe green berries; they can't wait for them to turn red.

Everyday in the Forest

In the past and even today, children love to roam around outdoors more than adults.

Being around trees and forests is fun, but it is important to know what to do and what not to do. For example, only certain fruits are edible, and others are poisonous. People have learnt this from experience, and children from their elders.

Thorns

When children graze cattle or goats in the forest, they look for the Sindi berry tree. The berries are delicious, and the children snack on them. Birds and monkeys love these berries too. You can make juice from the berries, but they're just good to eat by themselves.

The thorns of the Sindi tree are really **sharp**. If you get pricked by one, you suffer the whole day. Sindi twigs make good brooms.

Knowing what to eat

We eat the leaves of the Gondhi tree. We wait for the first buds to appear on the tree. Soon, they fall off, leaving the fruit behind. I've shown those buds here, they're really tasty. People eat these leaves like spinach. Not just human beings, animals like them too, specially monkeys. We cook the leaves in yoghurt or tamarind, in something sour.

People know edible leaves from poisonous ones. Children who graze cattle or goats in the forest eat these buds and fruits as snacks. They climb up the tree and pluck them, with the animals grazing below. How did people first begin to eat these leaves? The shamans are said to be the first people who ate them. Children watch their parents, and they know what is good to eat.

Tree Matters

You might think that when people are around trees and forests, they know them so well that they don't notice them after a while. But the Bhils have a special way of relating to trees: trees are not only useful to them, but also symbols of great beauty. Trees make the forest a home, a place of protection and a place of inspiration.

Tree Designs

Our tattoo designs are based on the shape of the Ryan tree, and so I've shown it in the form of a popular tattoo design.

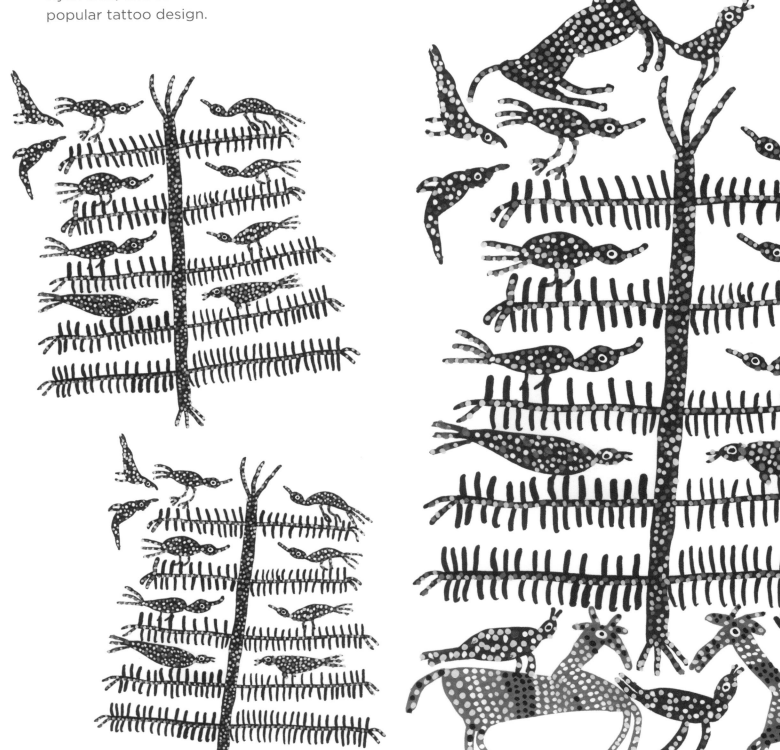

There are goats trying to climb the tree. They love the leaves; people can eat these leaves too. There are lovely fruits on this tree, you can see them from far away. They make a good snack when you're in the forest.

The Birth of Jangal

This is the story of my friend Bhuri Bai, who gave birth to a child in the jungle. It was about eleven in the morning, and Bhuri Bai had come to work. We were clearing some land near the forest. Bhuri Bai was pregnant, and felt a little uncomfortable. She decided to go home, and started making her way slowly through the trees. We saw her sitting under some bushes and hurried over.

Bhuri Bai was in **pain**...

The baby was being born already!

We helped her give birth, and brought some water to wash her and the child.

I named the boy **Jangal.**

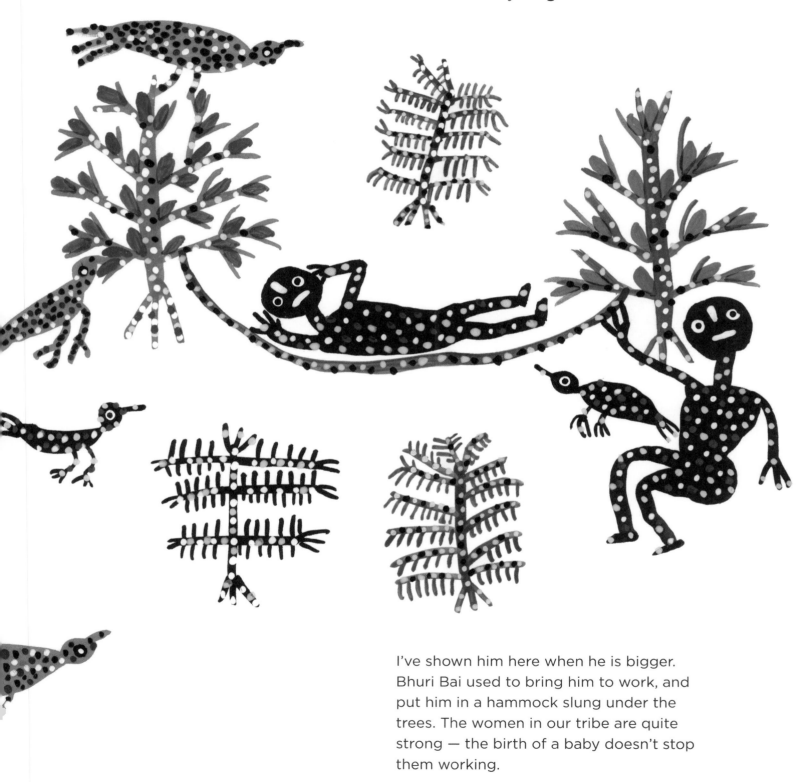

I've shown him here when he is bigger. Bhuri Bai used to bring him to work, and put him in a hammock slung under the trees. The women in our tribe are quite strong — the birth of a baby doesn't stop them working.

Guardians and Gods

A forest can be a dangerous place. The Bhils aren't afraid of venturing into the jungle, yet they know they need to be mindful of what they do. They think of the forest as containing spirits that are both dangerous and protective.

Secrets and Mysteries

The Chudel is a mischievous jungle spirit. It can frighten you, and people do get scared, but it won't really harm you. It is around both during the day and at night when everyone's asleep.

When you're roaming around, it can enter you, and then you need to appease it, give it what it asks for.

Here is someone who has been taken by the spirit. It's very demanding, and once you fulfill its demands, it lets you go.

I've shown a boy and a girl beneath the Chudel tree. There is a traditional Bhil story about these runaways, who hide in the hollow of this tree. It's a huge tree, with many hollows to hide in. You can still see such trees only in our forests.

Mother of the Forest

This is the goddess of the jungle. She lives deep in the forest and protects those who go in there. We need to venture in deep when we gather firewood for food. We don't take anything that's still green and alive, only dry twigs.

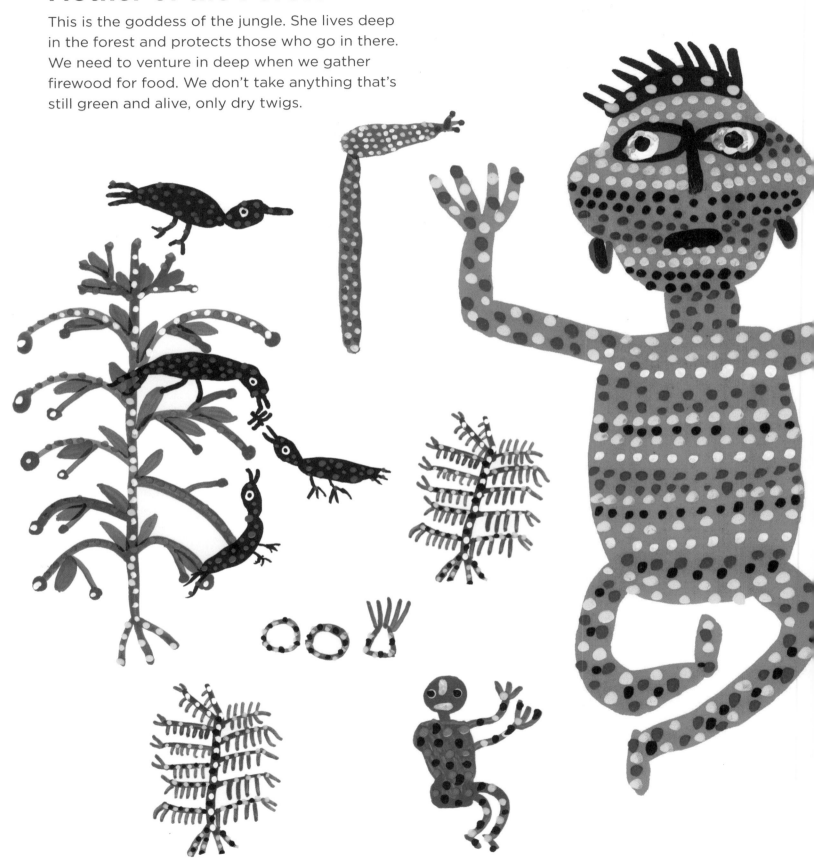

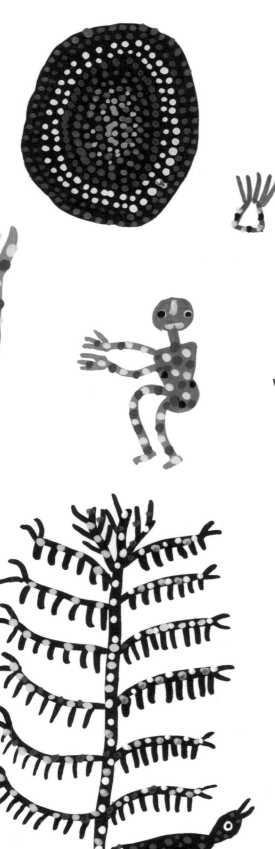

A forest is a dangerous place, many bad things can happen to you:

poisonous thorns...

losing your way...

wild animals...

snakes...

The Mother protects us, she allows us to eat. She guides us through the places that have dead wood.

People mark her presence with a stone — stones are gods and goddesses too! A stone, and a flag: that's all it takes to make a tribal temple.

Lost and Found

The god Kasumer lives in the jungle. He lives under the tree. He helps people who've lost their way and those who suffer because of ill-luck. People who are possessed by bad spirits also pray to him.

People make a vow to Kasumer: if he fulfills their wishes, they promise to worship him, and give him offerings. Each does what he or she wants or can afford. So, some of us worship him by offering coconuts. Others bring a chicken to him.

You often find clay horses around Kasumer's shrine. This is because some people take a vow that they will build a temple if their wish comes true... these are poor people, so they can't build grand temples, only modest statues made of clay.

These are the horses.

We've started dotting everything...

and so the horses too... !

Badadev the Great God

This is a banyan tree, under which we seat Badadev, our Great God. He is in the form of a stone.

People in the village seek him out under the tree, and worship him.

They ask for **boons**, or for a way out of their troubles.

There is a platform around the banyan tree in a village, where people sit around and talk.

Trees for Every Occasion

The forest stops being a fearful place once a person gets to know it: Bhils connect to the forest through trees. The trees that are in the forest are also in their neighbourhoods. Trees are central to everything they do, and they have their favourite trees for every occasion.

The Wedding Party

This is a wedding in our village. The bridegroom's party has walked all the way from their village across the forest. Now they've been seated under a Mango tree, near a field.

There are musicians around them, playing different instruments.

This reception is part of the wedding ceremony and if a bride's household does not have a Mango tree near their field, they will ask their neighbours if they can seat the groom's party under their tree.

Mango and Mahua are considered auspicious trees. The trees to be avoided are bitter ones, such as the Neem or thorny trees with berries.

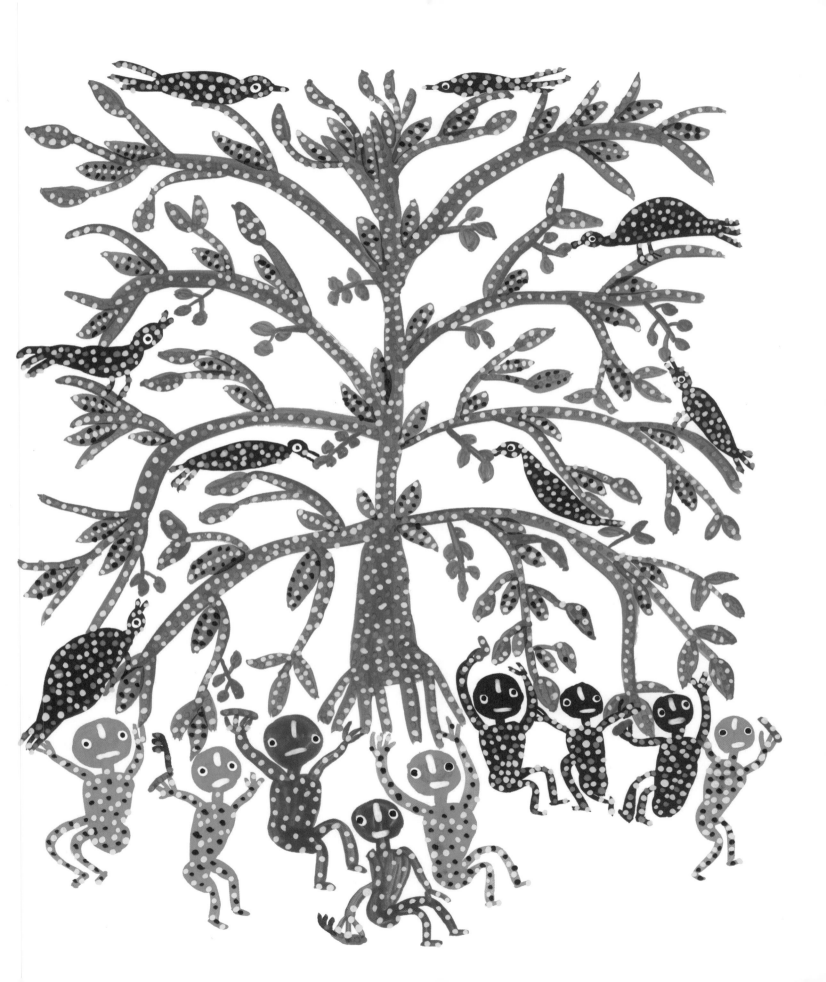

Bitter Medicine

The bitter Neem is an important medicinal tree, very useful in many ways. It's bitter and cool: effective for all kinds of diseases...

Neem oil kills worms and lice. The leaves are used to lightly brush children with measles, the twigs make excellent toothbrushes.

It's good for all occasions except one: **we'd never let a wedding party rest under a Neem tree!**

The bitterness of the Neem is considered inauspicious... and a marriage shouldn't start on a bitter note.

Khakra Leaves

The Khakra tree is central to tribal life (along with Mahua). We use the leaf on all festive occasions: from birth to death. A newborn's arrival is celebrated with a meal served on Khakra leaves. A wedding feast is served on Khakra leaves.

For every prayer and ceremony, offerings are placed on Khakra leaves. **Seven people are fed.**

It's a large dense tree, and if someone hides in there, you can't see them. The leaves come out after April. When the leaves shed, in summer, the tree bursts into red flowers... and you can see it from really far away.

I haven't shown the flowers because this tree has leaves. You can't have both together. There is a variety of Khakra with white flowers, but it's really rare.

Mahua, the Tree of Life

This is one of the most important trees in tribal life. Mahua flowers are used to distil a liquor that is sacred to us. We drink it ceremoniously, and on all occasions from birth to death. There is no festivity or ritual without Mahua.

You can't buy this drink anywhere, people brew it at home. The flowers fall around July. People set out to gather fallen flowers. There is an oil that is extracted from the Mahua. We use it as medicine. Mahua flowers are like money for us. People take them to the market and trade them for other things they need, such as rice or dal.

A palm season

This is the toddy palm, from which toddy is made. A pot is tied to the tree, to tap the liquid from the palm fruit.

This man is climbing the tree to tap toddy.

This is done once a year, during the cold season. You can drink it fresh, or leave it to ferment and become liquor.

You cannot keep toddy for too long, it turns sour.

Here are people drinking toddy. **One of them has had too much!**

You can eat the fruit too. It's white and very tender. It needs to be young, old fruits are hard.

Celebration

The Holi festival is one of the most important celebrations in our village. There are fairs and carnivals, and people throw colours at each other.

Just after the festival, young girls get together and go from house to house, asking for gifts from people who have come into good fortune:

a newborn

a good harvest

a new house

They get Mahua to drink in each household they visit, and become really merry. People give them gifts and money. At the end of the day, the girls sit down happily under a Jamun tree and divide up the money they've collected.

I think I will leave the girls to their counting, and end my story. Holi has come and gone but I have work to do. Time to say goodbye!

Gangu Bai belongs to an indigenous community called Bhil, whose members live in villages across western and central India. Her rich repertoire of stories is steeped in the community's lore. The award-winning artist has been painting for over two decades, and her work has been exhibited both in India as well as abroad. Gangu works with the National Museum of Mankind in Bhopal.

The origins of Bhil art go back to the festive and decorative designs made by women on the floors and walls of homes. Called 'mittichitra' — literally 'mud painting' — this relief work was made up of ornamental patterns, birds and animals. The dots that characterise Bhil paintings came from the tradition of decorating animals with dotted patterns, using natural dyes and powders. Bhil art has since evolved into a joyful style of painting, typically featuring a teeming world shared equally by human beings, animals and plants. The art moved to canvas and paper in the 1970s, when a contemporary artist worked with a group of Bhil women and suggested that they work on a different surface. Acrylic colours gradually replaced pigments made of natural substances.

The Bhils were once hunter-gatherers, but became cultivators over time. Today some of them have moved to cities, and many work in factories and mines, but their sense of themselves is strongly connected to the memory of being forest people. Gangu Bai's work celebrates this connection with nature, and the rituals associated with it.

Gangu worked with Tara Books for over two weeks to create this book. We were enchanted with her vivacious art, which seemed both archaic and startlingly modern. Listening to her tales of Bhil life, we suggested that she work on a set of paintings based on her memories of growing up with trees. Gangu came up with stories and paintings featuring particular trees. Building on this, we constructed a narrative out of her art and the tree tales she told us. We hope *Tree Matters* captures the intimate, yet playful relationship that Gangu — and other Bhil women — have with the natural world. To us, the book unfolds as painted ecological wisdom, lightly held, but, nonetheless, a testimony to sustainable everyday living.